HYMNS OF PRUDENTIUS

HYMNS OF PRUDENTIUS

The *Cathemerinon;* or, *The Daily Round*

BY Aurelius Prudentius Clemens

TRANSLATED BY DAVID R. SLAVITT

THE JOHNS HOPKINS UNIVERSITY PRESS
BALTIMORE AND LONDON

© 1996 The Johns Hopkins University Press
All rights reserved. Published 1996
Printed in the United States of America on acid-free paper
05 04 03 02 01 00 99 98 97 96   5 4 3 2 1

The Johns Hopkins University Press
2715 North Charles Street
Baltimore, Maryland 21218-4319
The Johns Hopkins Press Ltd., London

ISBN 0-8018-5412-1

Library of Congress Cataloging-in-Publication Data
will be found at the end of this book.

A catalog record for this book is available from the British Library.

For Kelly Cherry and Margaret Boeth

CONTENTS

INTRODUCTION

What in the world could have drawn a skeptical Jewish aesthete of the late twentieth century to these devout poems of a fourth-century Christian?

It is not an altogether impossible connection. First, let us consider the phrase I planted in that initial sentence. "What in the world . . . ?" is Prudentius's strategic discovery. It may have been Archimedes who talked about how, with a place to stand, he could move the world. But Prudentius understood how the terra firma could be made into an almost endless series of occasions for the consideration of loftier and more spiritual things. Given a place to stand, Prudentius will levitate and soar.

The contemplative exercises of St. François de Sales and of St. Ignatius are, fundamentally, codifications of the practice of Prudentius. These three-step calisthenics of the spirit involved a contemplation of place, an act of analysis, and a reformation of the spirit in an exertion of the will or judgment. As Louis Martz observed some years ago, these meditative practices informed the poetry of George Herbert and John Donne, both of whom I was lucky enough to encounter early and with excellent guides. They were important in my education and development as a poet. To their work I have continually returned and repaired. And when I saw how Prudentius had prefigured and enabled their poetry, I felt a pleasant recognition, even a degree of kinship.

It is also true that Prudentius, as a Christian, was looking back on the classical world with feelings of affectionate yearning not unlike my own. When I undertook the Englishing of Ovid's poetry of exile and his *Metamorphoses,* I imagined myself as believing in his gods and their miracles. I don't, of course. Few of us do. Still, as readers and translators, we can entertain such beliefs. I can, when reading Prudentius, pretend to a faith that even to a skeptic is comforting and nourishing.

Prudentius's Ovid and my own, I fancied, might not be utter strangers. And there is, without question, a lot of Ovid in Prudentius. His exempla are Ovidian in their inventiveness and occasional preening. He delights in authorial intrusion and the way he can contrive authority from it, the dazzle of his display serving as an index of his enthusiasm and of the reader's, too.

His devout Christianity is foreign to me more because of its devotion than anything else. If we are comfortable with Ovid's and Virgil's pantheon, that may be because we have tamed those gods and no longer see them as a threat. (There are, at any rate, no fundamentalist pagans with political agendas.) The Olympians are mythological beings, but the Christian God is still very much in business, so that it would be tactless to refer to Christian "mythology."

Putting it another way, it was a Christian society I grew up in. I have learned to define myself—as I think many Jews do—not only as positively *this* but, in a more strenuously negative way, as *not that*. We don't do Christmas; we don't do Easter. No trees and no bunnies— even though these are not actually Christian emblems.

Many years ago, I was in the boys choir of the Mamaroneck Avenue School in White Plains and, in a black choir robe with a white surplice, sang Latin carols at the Christmas assemblies. This would probably not be permitted today, but it wasn't altogether a bad thing. I didn't believe the carols, but they were beautiful, and we sang them reasonably well. I remember that experience with some fondness, as I remember compulsory chapel at Andover, where I first heard the organ music of Bach and Buxtehude in recessionals that almost made up for John Kemper's hectoring and Graham Baldwin's blather. Now I can look at the Madonnas and Pietás, listen to masses and Stabat Maters, or read Dante and Prudentius and Herbert and Donne as I learned to do back then, not for religious reasons but purely as a connoisseur, which, of course, involves my looking at them *as if* . . .

We contrive whatever responses we can to these complicated occasions and discover that we'd have been impoverishing ourselves if we hadn't. It is Prudentius's confidence and generosity, I think, that I find most appealing. If he could cross confessional boundaries to read and digest the pagans, I can read him. As an outsider, I may even have certain advantages, because the machinery of these hymns is not so familiar to me as it would be to a practicing Christian. What was fresh then, because Prudentius was inventing it, is fresh to me, because I am looking at the rhetoric with an interest that is part anthropological and part craftsmanly.

Prudentius's Latin is decorative and his poetic stance is enormously appealing. I have tried to do the voice and suggest to others something of what I admire in it. If I read these poems as objets d'art, I have no objection to my Christian friends reading them another way, as devotions. Indeed, I cannot for the life of me guess which of us will be getting more out of them. The particular belief is perhaps not so much the crucial issue as the yearning for belief—for the faithful feel, in the momentary flaggings of their faith, a fervent longing most agnostics have experienced, whether they admit it or not.

What I found immediately engaging in Prudentius was his combination of literary and cultural sophistication with a spiritual simplicity or even naiveté. To beseech God the Father, one reverts to the candor and directness of that child one wishes one had been. There is a purely technical aspect to this paradoxical stance. It is a version of the pastoral, I think, albeit one that Empson never addressed, and it suggests the odd effects some composers get by using boy sopranos to meet their complicated musical needs. Whatever Gordian knot of intellectual complexity the artist may propound for our consideration, this artistic stratagem offers the hope that purity of heart will somehow help. Talent, intelligence, sophistication, and erudition are elitist; honesty and innocence are just as rare but they seem less exclusive and more democratic. Prudentius's implicit appeal to an entirely different set of values is, at the very least, a magician's gesture of distraction. His insistence on the importance of the simple virtues is what allows him to be as brilliant and complicated as he likes in his literary techniques without running any risk of offending us.

•   •   •

Prudentius was born in Spain in the consulship of Salia, that is, in A.D. 348, either at Saragossa (Caesaraugusta), Tarragona (Tarraco), or Calahorra (Calagurris). He was, therefore, six years older than Augustine, and he was thirteen when Julian, the last pagan emperor, came to the throne and attempted to suppress Christianity and restore paganism.* Upon Julian's death in 363, Jovian succeeded him, only to be quickly replaced by Valentinian, who divided the empire with his brother Valens. These co-emperors were both Christians. Valentinian, in the West, established a court at Trier that included such men as Jerome, Ausonius (who became tutor to Valentinian's son, Gratian), and Martin of Tours.

In the prefatory verses to his collected poems, which he brought out in his fifty-seventh year, Prudentius lets

---

*Gore Vidal's novel *Julian* (Boston, 1964) is a lively source of information about this curious character and his times.

us know that he prepared for a career in the law and moved from that into some post in civil administration, probably under the emperor Theodosius. He was, then, a public servant who wrote poetry, like St. John Perse, Basil Bunting, and George Seferis—or Prior, Ralegh, and Chaucer, for that matter.

He seems to have traveled a good deal, had been to Rome, and was in touch with the other poets of his time, Ausonius and the younger court poet Claudian. He was probably also familiar with the Christian poetry of Ambrose and Paulinus and the epigrams of Pope Damasus.

That his work is included in Catholic prayer books is a mixed blessing. Although the church has provided him steadily with readers, they haven't always been his ideal audience. Fragments of Hymns 1 and 2 are found today in the Roman breviary: *Ales diei nuntius, Lux ecce surgit aurea* and *Nox et tenebrae, et nubila* for Tuesday, Wednesday, and Thursday at Lauds; Hymn 12 was the source of *Quicumque Christum quaeritis* for the Feast of the Transfiguration of Our Lord, *O sola magnarum urbium* for Epiphany, and *Audit tyrranus anxius* and *Salvete flores martyrum* for Holy Innocents. In the introduction to her translation *Prudentius' Hymns,** Sister M. Clement Eagan,

*(Washington, D.C., 1962).

C.C.V.I., informs us that "other hymns of the *Cathe-merinon* found their way, in part or as a whole, into the Mozarabic Breviary. The hymn *Inventor rutilis dux bone luminis* for Vespers of the first Sunday after the Octave of Epiphany is taken from Hymn 5. The hymn *Cultor Dei memento* for Compline is taken from *Cathemerinon* 6, the hymn before sleep. Hymn 7, for the times of fasting, is used in its entirety for the Hours of Terce, Sext, and None during Lent. The hymn *Psallat altitudo coeli,* for Vespers of the Sunday within the Octave of Easter, consists of twenty-four lines from the *Cathemerinon* 9. The rest of this hymn in sections is used for Vespers from Monday to Saturday of Easter week and for the Feast of the Ascension. The hymn *Deus ignee fons animarum* for the Vespers of the Office of the Dead is composed of forty-four lines from Hymn 10, plus an added stanza not found in any of the manuscripts and a doxology."

My sense that this may not have been unalloyed good news for Prudentius's reputation as a poet comes from her remarks later on about how "any estimate of Prudentius must include a recognition of certain defects in his works, notably the length and prolixity of his hymns, the crude realism in his descriptions of the torments of the martyrs, the long declamatory speeches, the unreality of his allegory, and his excessive use of alliteration and assonance. Though his writings as a whole cannot be ranked among those of the greatest poets, they do not fall far short of great poetry in many instances . . . Prudentius has . . . greater claims to greatness, however, in the Christian thought and inspiration of his poetry." A recent critic has declared with truth that Prudentius is "first a Catholic and only in the second place a poet."*

What can I say, except that this isn't how I see him? The good sister's appraisal was not at all heterodox or even eccentric and reflects fairly the judgment of the nineteenth century and the early part of the twentieth. It took English departments a generation or so before the revival of metaphysical poetry caught on and spread through the academy. The tastes of the classics faculties tend to be even more leisurely in the pace of their readjustments.

That question, though, of the priorities of Prudentius's poetry and his Catholicism seems odd to me. I am more comfortable with Peter Brown's formulation in

*F.J.E. Raby, *A History of Christian Latin Poetry from the Beginnings to the Close of the Middle Ages,* 2d ed. (Oxford, 1953), 47.

Society and the Holy in Late Antiquity,* which does not oppose Christianity to paganism, or religion to art, but resembles more closely what I have myself experienced in a Christian society: "For the men of Late Antiquity, the classical past—and especially the gods who hung so close to them in the planets and in the heavy clusters of the Milky Way—were not yet 'the past.' It was not an option that could be 'revived' or 'abandoned'; 'applied' or 'deemed irrelevant.' It was part of the air that men breathed and it is incautious to assume precipitately that, any more than in classical China or in the Islamic world, this mellow air did not contain most of the elements necessary for continual, healthy respiration."

Theodosius's time was a relatively tranquil one for late antiquity, and Prudentius's view of the world was optimistic—it has been called "triumphalism." Claudian's view, a much darker one, turned out to be correct. His *Rape of Proserpine* is an omen of ruin, an elegant fragment that passed itself off as a merely literary exercise while it rehearsed the central myth of the old, and by now proscribed, mystery cults. It was the swan song of classical culture and religion. Prudentius's lines, in *Cathemerinon* 3, sound much more sanguine:

*(Berkeley, 1982), 93.

sperne, Camena, leves hederas,
cingere tempora quis solita es,
sertaque mystica dactylico
texere docta liga strophio,
laude Dei redimita comas.

(3.26–30)

Literally, he is telling his muse to put away the light ivy she uses to crown her brow and learn to weave mystic garlands and bind them with a ribbon of dactyls. She should decorate her hair with the praise of God. It is a Pindaric topos he has adapted, or, anyway, Horatian (Horace was himself Pindaric). The work of the earlier poets provides Prudentius with some of the bright strands he uses now, weaving his new garland.

This is more catholic than Catholic (although that isn't a distinction that would have made any sense to him). The fall of Rome, shortly after Prudentius's death, does not diminish the importance of his suave and civilized demeanor. The world, as we keep relearning, is not a reasonable place, but the moral imperative remains nevertheless to behave as if it were.

HYMNS OF PRUDENTIUS

I
HYMN FOR COCKCROW

"Coco rico," the rooster crows.
The dawn is come, and he sings to those
who lie abed. So Christ does, too,
rousing our sluggish souls to the new
     dawn of His being.
Beds are for bodily sickness or sloth,
but the sun is up, and now God's truth
shines in the skies, as birds declare
from rooftops into the morning air
     the glory of seeing.

Let every daybreak symbolize
the falling away of scales from eyes
hungry for light, as all our souls
shall be when the bell of judgment tolls,
     and we repent.
These darknesses we now rehearse

we then shall understand and curse,
mortified by our wretched torpor,
and begging divine forgiveness for poor
　　　　lives misspent.

The dawn air breathes a promise we
delight to hear—that misery
and sin may vanish as some bad dream.
Miraculous, morning may yet redeem
　　　　our grievous sins.
The phantoms that roam the world at night
know this and therefore abhor the light
of God's creation that purifies.
They flee to the murk and hide their eyes
　　　　when the day begins.

We snuggle in our warm beds and snore
though heaven is what we have prayed for
all night, as fervent as Peter who
our Savior said would be untrue
　　　　before cockcrow
three times. He yearned for day to break,
retract, undo his grave mistake—
or mortal weakness, let us say.

(In the kinder, clearer light of day
      he'd not have done so

wicked a thing, or said what he said.)
At cockcrow Christ returned from the dead.
It was, therefore, at just this hour
that death in its all but limitless power
      was overthrown.
The pouring down of heaven's graces
into our spirits' darkest spaces
is figured when we first glimpse the light
to which we've arrived in hell's despite.
      Having been shown

such wonders, let us learn to call
on Jesus, that He may save us all,
rousing our sluggish hearts from sleep.
We pray, we meditate, we weep
      in deep chagrin,
for the blind pursuit of earthly glory,
money, and all the hallucinatory
pleasures, the goods of the world of men.
Wake us from such vain dreams and then
      gather us in.

Under the blankets, the body's heat
is cozy. Still, we must plant our feet
on the floor and stand, in an act of will
and also faith that in this still
            immaculate day
we may begin afresh and do
what enlightened virtue tells us to.
The sun is risen! On the earth
birds exult in the great rebirth;
            give thanks and pray.

II
MORNING HYMN

An endless night, obfusc and shrouded
so that even our thoughts are roiled and clouded . . .
But then in a gentling of the air
the sky relents and our despair
lifts as if Christ were come again,
returning to the hearts of men
the colors of hope and, in restoration
of every subtle tint and hue,
repairing for us the Lord's creation.

In the recklessness of unbelief,
villains consort, killer and thief,
who dread the coming on of dawn.
When light and right shall set upon
them, fugitives and paramours
repent as pimps console their whores
who feel the pangs of their chagrin.

Hung-over, bleary-eyed and slow,
they recognize their state of sin
and flinch as if to avoid a blow.

They look about them at the good
men busy with decent work that should
be done: the businessman, the farmer,
store-clerk, sailor, soldier in armor
are doing their duty, every one
rising with the rising sun,
while we who love the Lord devote
ourselves to prayer: on bended knees,
we chant the matins, and each note
ascends into a sweetened breeze.

Oh, let the sun's rays penetrate
the murkiest heart and cleanse the great
foulness within the soul of man,
as once the Jordan's water ran
to purify us. Do this thing
again for us each day, O King.
Turn pitch to crystal, and coal white
as milk. It is in blackness' grip

that Jacob and the angel fight,
writhe on the ground, smite thigh and hip,

but then as the dawn restores the field,
will the burly angel, generous, yield.
We too, each morning, weak, arise;
our strength returns; we rub our eyes
and look about beneath the blue
sky of the morning, hoping to
pass the whole day untainted, free
from sins of word and deed, for we know
a blazing eye looks down to see
how we behave ourselves below.

III
HYMN BEFORE MEALS

O sweet Christ, who bore the cross,
the word made flesh, our holy light
brighter than stars, shine down on us
and bless our bodies' appetite

for You are nourishment, our sweet
and salt, our spice. Unless the Lord
leaven our bread and flavor our meat,
we take no pleasure at His board

whereon is spread our feast. My muse
must put the ivy leaves away
of classic epicures and use
her metric elegance to pray

in thanks to the Lord and sing His praise.
What better employment could she find

than to reflect the dazzling rays
of heaven that, seen directly, blind?

The fruits of the earth, those bounties which
the Lord has set before us, we
receive dismayed — the gifts are rich
beyond our poor deserving. He

has given us the fowler's snares
and taught the fisherman his skill
with nets and hooks. The vine that bears
clusters of grapes that summers fill

with juice, He gives, and then the wine.
He cultivates the tree whose sprig
is the sign of peace and from whose fine
fruit we make oil. Our debt is big,

and, grateful, we should be content
with these things our gentle Lord supplies
for us — He surely never meant
that we should slaughter beasts whose cries

turn any feast to funeral wake.
Take milk and cheese and honey. Fill
the ravening belly, for God's sake,
with fruits and greens and grains as will

sustain us well, and we shall feel
at peace with nature. Be the guest
of the Lord who is host of every meal,
which as communion He has blessed.

Let us sing His praises then,
for we have seen the summer squall
shaking the tree that gives to men
beneath it riches surpassing all

imagination, freely strewn,
bejeweled with raindrops, on the ground.
Play then the lyres' ancient tune
and let the trumpeters resound

in the celebration of each day,
its gifts of morning vigor and
of sweet fatigue as light gives way
and we can experience the grand

restoration of body and soul
of a good dinner, where He who first
made man from clay repairs us all:
for Him we hunger, for Him we thirst.

With the voice and breath of my flesh and bones,
let me rejoice in my Creator,
and sing out in resonating tones
that from every hillside echo the greater

glory of God who made the fields,
the streams, the woodlands, and gave to men
this rich domain and all it yields.
A paradise it was, but then

the serpent came to beguile the heart
of innocence, and the woman ate
the forbidden fruit, which was the start
of all our woes. Expatriate,

not only from nature but from their own
bodies, the man and woman, in shame,
covered themselves, and everyone
since then has been tainted by that same

sinfulness for which we pay
the heavy price of mortality,
the imperfection of that clay
of which we are fashioned. But One who was free

of any flaw descended from
the heavens, embodied the word of the Father
in living flesh, our Savior, come
not from some conjugal bed but rather

the womb of a virgin worthy to make
war on that viper again and put
her heel on the head of the vile snake.
Coiling and writhing beneath her foot

it spews its venom in vain, the green
poison lost on the green lawn . . .
And what can this puzzling portent mean?
Must beasts of prey now learn to fawn

on savage sheep? In the skies above
will eagles flock together and flee
the depredations of the dove?
O Christ, be Thou that dove for me.

You are the snow-white lamb in whose
presence the wolf and tiger, too,
are thunderstruck, as Your grace subdues
all violence. We ask that You,

good God, may hear our fervent prayer:
refresh us modestly and sustain
our bodies with calibrated care.
From gluttony, help us refrain,

as from immoderate drinking. Food
and wine, in proper measure, are
God's gifts to us and meant for good,
but the tempting serpent is never far

away. He takes the gluttons in,
seducing as he once did Eve.
Protect us from that kind of sin,
who trust in You as we believe

that You will one day resurrect
our frail flesh and from coffins take
our mouldering dust, which You'll perfect
and bring home for sweet Jesus' sake.

IV

HYMN AFTER MEALS

Now that we have nourished bodies,
    let us likewise feed our souls
and set these mouths that chew and swallow
    to other, more important goals—

the framing of our songs of praise to
    God the Father on His throne
among the cherubs and the seraphs.
    He is supreme, the Lord, alone,

with neither ending nor beginning.
    He is the *fons et origo*
of everything that is, instilling
    faith and virtue here below.

Life He gives and then salvation,
    through which comes immortality

in heaven's precincts where His spirit
      reigns in light and purity.

Into the bosom's temple of those
      who keep His image enshrined therein,
He enters, but departs forthwith
      should there be any taint of sin

to offend Him. He has made provision
      for body and for spirit, too.
The moderation at the table
      we practice will at once renew

the soul's robustness and sustain
      the flesh, its vessel. Thus, the Lord
kept Daniel in that den of lions
      safe from their cruel jaws. No sword

he had, but only faith: he would not
      bow to the idols of Babylon.
The lions nuzzle him, purr like kittens,
      lick his outstretched hand, and fawn.

A splendid pose! But all in nature
   changes over time: we feel
our bodies' promptings. The peckish hero
   looks to heaven for his next meal,

and heaven answers his prayer. An angel
   descends to earth. By design or luck,
not far away, to feed his farm-hands,
   the kindly prophet, Habakkuk,

is bringing out the noon repast.
   The angel lifts him and they sail
giddily through the air together.
   He clutches still that dinner pail.

The angel sets him down in Daniel's
   den. Together, they break bread
and eat what the gracious Lord has given.
   "Praise Him," each of those worthies said,

as we should, too, who here, together,
   thank God for these His gifts this day.
Imprisoned in this world of violence,
   surrounded by fierce beasts of prey,

we look to Him for our protection.
From every quarter, set upon,
afflicted, harried, we look to heaven,
and the fearsome lion's wrath is gone.

Eat hearty, then, of the Lord's provision.
Do not take dainty nibbles, but
wolf down the grain of truth, the food
that fed the virtue of prophets. What

is sweeter, more delicious? What
is better for our health? The word
of God will protect from any lions
those who trust in Christ the Lord.

V

HYMN AT LAMP LIGHTING

The night comes on; the day is done —
that alternation was begun

when first the Lord declared aloud
"Let there be light," and from a cloud

fixed the times and seasons that He
repeats for us punctiliously,

who in our apprehension turn
to Christ to be our lantern: Burn,

kindling faith in us. Starlight
may ornament the skies at night,

and the moon, at times, make our path clear.
But You are our lamp with whom we fear

no evil. With You we have steel
and flint, and oil and wicks. We'd feel

our way in menacing darkness, grope
in apprehension, but for the hope

we have of You. The gloom of night
descends outside; this room is bright

with torches' flames and sweet beeswax
candles. Moses, in his tracks,

stopped, astonished by the flame
that left the bush untouched. That same

holy incandescence led
his people who from Pharaoh fled

across the windswept desert. We
think of these mercies when we see

figured in every candle's glow
those miracles of long ago.

The Egyptian is prepared for war,
gives chase, makes haste, but at the shore

of the Red Sea, to which the guide
has led his people, waves divide.

The Pharaoh rushes forward. He
and his host are drowned together. The sea

covers their helmeted heads. Their cries
are dreadful. Random fragments rise

of their equipment, flotsam, sad
reminders of the suffering bad

kings can impose and are subject to.
Let us thank God and praise anew

the power of Christ our Savior, speak
in reverence of how He protects the weak,

and tell our children once more how
from the barren flint the water's flow

quenched the thirst of desperate men
and women in that desert. Then,

He pours down manna from the sky,
and at Marah,* where the people cry

that the water is bitter, He supplies
a log to sweeten it. In this wise,

He cares for us with quail blown in
by the winds to the Wilderness of Sin.

Such acts of mercy continue, are
perhaps not so spectacular,

but save our lives — as the sailor learns
when the salt spray flies and the green sea churns

and his boat pitches and yaws. He dreams
of grassy hillsides and gentle streams

*Exodus 15:23.

where marigolds and violets grow.
Heaven it is, as all of us know

in our hearts, that homeland that one day we
may hope to return to, where we'll see

with our own eyes those precincts where
roses and cinnamon scent the air.

We'll hear the blessed chorus sing
such hymns as make our own hearts ring

in harmony and delight, while they
who live in hell have a holiday

from torment, as when God before
came back from Acheron's black shore.

Into the deepest gloom of night
the morning star brings glints of light

rekindling hopes and repairing the loss
of those who mourn for the Lord's cross.

In churches, on Easter eve, we burn
candles all night, eager to turn

that dark to day when the sun will rise
as did our Lord, the light of our eyes

and hearts and souls. Through Christ, we see.
Night falls, but we have courage. We

bless the anointing unction, this,
the oil of our lamps. Its glory is His.

We honor Him and thank the giver
of light, the threefold God, forever.

VI

HYMN BEFORE SLEEP

Father, be with me, and Christ, the word made flesh,
and You, the Holy Spirit, watch over me now.
The tasks of the day are finished at last. To refresh
my tired limbs, I lay me down. My brow

unfurrows, as my mind lets troubles go
and I commence to float on oblivion's current.
I think of the Lord's mercy, providing so
for repair of our wearying, wearisome bodies that
    weren't

designed to soar as our minds can do in flights
not unlike angels' arabesques, when we take
the heavenly view of dreams, which is why our nights
can be far brighter than what we know, awake,

as if the dome of the skies had opened wide
and we, transfixed in the unaccustomed glare,

could see the truth of our lives. We are terrified
or else encouraged by what we've confronted there.

In ancient days in Egypt, wise Joseph read
the dreams in prison of Pharaoh's seneschal
and baker, and to each of them he said
what good or evil thing would soon befall.

When Pharaoh in three days restored the one
and hanged the other high, and Joseph's skill
was proven — he'd foretold what would be done —
the King sent for him, asking of him, "Will

you read my dream as well, of the seven fat
and the seven lean kine that came to devour them?"
Joseph unraveled the hidden meaning of that —
a famine was imminent. His stratagem

was the storing up of grain. The Pharaoh set
Joseph beside him as viceroy to share
in the rule of the kingdom. And in our sleep, even yet,
is where the Lord at times may choose to declare

His deepest mysteries and make them plain
for us to understand. The evangel John

was sleeping. To his visionary brain
came vivid dreams that we still ponder on,

of the Lamb of the Thunderer, dripping piteous
  blood,
who can alone unseal the sacred book;
His sword is two-edged and both ways are good;
He holds the keys in His hand; He keeps the lock.

To Him the illustrious Father has assigned
the seat of judgment for all eternity.
He fights the Antichrist and all his kind
and from those evil powers wrests victory.

The beast with that unfillable maw He sends
to the depths of hell, but the righteous man He saves
and gathers up to heaven. Whoso offends
by wicked deed, whose thought or dream depraves,

must turn to Him for mercy and forbearance.
Washed in the font, and touched with the holy oil,
we put our trust in Him at each appearance,
even in dreams, of the serpent. Christ will foil

his nefarious plans, protect us, and keep us pure
and worthy. Away, then, Satan! Back to your dim
recesses, for we lie down in bed, secure.
As we fall asleep, our thoughts shall be of Him.

VII
HYMN BEFORE FASTING

Child of the Virgin, Lord of the light
that shone in Bethlehem for us all,
be with us again today, and bless
our abstinence. We offer our small
      sacrifice — this fast,
        that we may be cleansed at last

of the body's foulness of fat and sweat
the intemperate flesh exudes. The mind
rebels, revolted, and learns to hate
that ravening that dulls the refined
      senses and coarsens the soul,
        distracting it from its goal.

We are able to pray all the better to God
after a fast. When the appetite
is subdued, the spirit has room to enlarge,

recover, and reassert its right.
     Long ago, in the desert spaces,
     far distant from any oasis,

the prophet Elijah fasted and prayed
in that silence in which the soul enjoys
an inspiring emptiness. One feels
the onset of a breathless poise,
     moment to moment the same,
     as the flesh melts away. There came

that flying chariot out of the sky
to bear that prophet on wings of the wind
and hold him high, a man at peace
above the corruption of those who had sinned.
     Moses, likewise, retires
     from appetites, lusts, and desires

for forty days and renounces the body's
perseverant promptings. His only meat
and drink are the tears that he lets fall
from his eyes. They dampen the dust at his feet.
     Prone on the ground he lies,
     as he hears the voice from the skies

of the living God. He trembles, afraid.
It resonates in his head and he closes
his eyes to the shimmering fire the Lord
is wearing that He may appear to Moses
      stretched out there on the sand
        on the way to the promised land.

John the Baptist also learned
at his mother's paps, shrunken and dry,
of hunger's gifts. Years later, when
he'd prophesied that, by and by,
      a virgin would come to birth
        with the Lord of all the earth,

he went in the shaggy skins of beasts
to live in the wilderness, supplied
with nothing. Deaf to the body's complaints,
he survived on what the land could provide—
      honeycombs from the bees,
        and locusts. Only from these

he took his nourishment. He washed
his body clean of the stains of sin,
as now men are baptized, reborn,

and the Holy Spirit comes rushing in
    like the pure water we pour,
    brighter than silver ore.

I will tell you another story — true,
but very strange, as Scripture can be —
of the tempering of the wrath of God
against that town of venery,
    endlessly seeking pleasure
    beyond all reason and measure.

In justice, they all deserved to die,
but mercy intervened. God gave
them another chance to amend their lives,
confess, repent, and thereby save
    their souls and the lives
    of their children and wives.

He called to Jonah to go and proclaim
His anger with Nineveh, warning them all
that this was their last chance to reform,
and, if they did not, their city would fall.
    "Go," the Almighty said
    to His servant — who thereupon fled

and embarked on a sailing vessel bound
for Tarshish. It soon cast off to sail
on a sea that grew rougher as winds picked up
in fury. The hearts of the sailors quail,
    and they try to determine who
      of the passengers or the ship's crew

might be cause of this turbulence, spinning a bottle
that points to the prophet. He is the one
they hurl overboard to drown in the deep.
When this act of purification is done,
    they can sail on, while he
      thrashes about in the sea,

where a monstrous fish that the Lord has sent
appears. It opens its gaping jaw
and swallows him whole. Jonah descends
through the gullet to land in the huge maw,
    fetid, slimy, and dark,
      of this whale or enormous shark.

He cannot tell, but three whole days
and nights elapse. He contrives to float
in the mess of the fish's stomach. At length,

the monster vomits him back up its throat
    and the creature then spits him
    back into the sea to swim

away, unharmed, to the nearby shore
where the waves break on a rocky beach.
Amazed to be whole and alive, he turns
his steps toward Nineveh, there to teach
    the people to mend their ways—
    "or the Lord, in a matter of days,"

he says, "will burn your city. Doubt
me not!" And now he can depart
to a mountaintop and sit on the ground,
watch, and wait for the flames to start.
    A plant that the Lord has made
    sprouts up to provide him shade.

Meanwhile, in Nineveh, fear of God
has seized the frivolous people at last.
They put on the garb of mourning, weep
and pray, and the men and women fast,
    begging forgiveness for
    those sins which they now abhor,

while the children roll in the dirt and wail
in fear. The king himself puts by
his jeweled crown and sprinkles his head
with ashes, while swaddled infants cry
       in hunger, but no wet nurse
       dares to invite God's curse.

The Lord looks down and is mollified
to see them suffer and hear their prayer.
He commutes His terrible sentence upon
all those who repented and fasted there.
       And we should likewise do
       as Jesus taught us to.

He who put on the burdens of flesh
with His mortal frame to consecrate
His heart went out to the desert to fast,
an act of the will that could moderate
       the heat of the body's fire
       and the tyrannies of desire.

That one the prophets of old had said
would come, our God, Emmanuel,
subdued these cravings that we feel, too,

amazing the foe who hoped to tell
    the world that this cannot
    be a god whom a woman begot,

but he is rebuked and, confounded, flees
behind Christ's back. Let us therefore
learn that lesson by which we may
turn with our lesser strengths to the more
    laudable goals and defy
    the vigilant enemy's sly

designs on us. With Christ our Lord
to guide and aid us, we will strive
to master our appetites that we
may let our inner spirits thrive
    and bloom in the devil's despite,
    free of unhealthy blight.

By this shall we earn the approval of Him
who rules the earth and the heavens above.
Our sacrifice may rouse our sluggish
faith and bestir our hearts to love
    Him who gave His Son
    for love of us, each one.

As surely as water will quench a blaze
or snow will melt when the sun burns,
so will our all-too-prominent faults
vanish as liberal faith returns.
       We shall clothe the naked and feed
       the hungry and those in need,

for we shall recall how rich and poor
are brothers nevertheless. We knew
this kinship all along, and yet
we failed to acknowledge that it was true.
       O Lord, amend our living
       and help us be rich in giving.

VIII
HYMN AFTER FASTING

Christ, our master, we, Your
servants over whom You
gently reign, give thanks: You
        taught us to restrain
the easily distracted
body, curb its whims, and
carry on the higher
        business of the brain.

Now that day is almost
done, we end our fasting
having met the obli-
        gations of our vow.
Grant, as we break bread that
our appetites be hearty,
and give us good digestion
        for our dinner now—

both in body and in
spirit. Keep us mindful
of what we have accomplished:
        Let us recall that poise
we knew when flesh conformed to
the promptings of the soul and
You allowed us glimpses
        of transcendental joys.

Exercises such as
this became our habit
when, as little children
        we started to obey
the dictates of our parents
to wash our hands and faces,
dress ourselves correctly,
        and comb our hair each day.

So we read in Matthew,*
who tells us, when we fast, to
maintain our good grooming.
        The point is not display

*6:16–18.

but private contemplation.
Our efforts at devotion
are meant for God the Father
           to whom alone we pray.

He, whose eye is on the
falling of each sparrow,
surely will take notice.
           No one else need know.
Watching after us, our
shepherd looks for laggard
lambs caught in the brambles,
           or lost, or merely slow.

He lifts them to His shoulders
and returns them to the flock still
grazing in the meadow.
           He cleans their wool of burs.
For the tenderness and care we
receive from our Creator,
let us be ever thankful,
           accepting what occurs

with grateful resignation.
We look to You to save us
in this world and the next and
        offer up our prayers
that never can begin to
equal what we owe You,
who feel it when we suffer
        and share in all our cares.

It is not fear that prompts us,
but a loving, true devotion.
We thank You when You feed us
        and make our bodies strong
with these dedicated morsels.
Nourish, too, our spirits;
give us that faith and courage
        for which all Christians long.

IX

HYMN FOR ANY HOUR

Fetch me a pen, lad. I mean to sing of the noble
deeds of Jesus Christ, the theme of my heavenly Muse.
For Him shall the lyre resound in the modes of the
    classic bards.
I invoke for my inspiration that same divine source
as once prompted the prophet who told us that He
    would come,
our God, made manifest, to teach mankind and save
    us.
What wonders have I to praise! Who on earth would
    deny
the miracles of His love? Our Alpha and our Omega,
the source and purpose and goal of all that was and is
or ever will be, His words created the air they rang
    on,
and heaven and earth and the seas of this tripartite
    world

as well as the sun and moon above it. He came to
    suffer
the pangs of mortal flesh that mankind might not
    perish,
to pay for us that debt of death our sins had incurred
and to save us all from hell. A virgin came to term
and brought forth a child conceived of the Holy
    Spirit, Him,
our blessed Redeemer, who showed us the face of the
    living God.
Let angels sing and the heavenly powers, while here
    below
we raise our voices, also, to join the harmonious
    consort,
each one of us whose despair He lifted from our sore
    hearts.
Let every inanimate object praise Him—as did the
    water
that changed in the tankards, to do His bidding, to
    vintage wine.
Not needing the brain's instruction or intervention,
    the body
hears His words and responds, as He orders that it be
    healed—

and the ulcerous festering flesh obeys the word of its
    Maker.

Eyes long buried in darkness, He has touched and
    opened,

restoring them to the light of the world. The leper's
    skin

He has cleansed, making it smooth. He has stilled the
    raging winds

and calmed the tormented seas. Even the touch of His
    garment

cures that woman who reached out her desperate
    hand, and . . . see!

her pallor is gone. Not even death itself can defy Him,

but He stands at the graveside, hears the desolate
    mother sob,

bids the young man, "Live!" and Lazarus leaves the
    tomb,

his decaying flesh revived, and breathes in fresh air
    again.

Christ walks upon water, and its fragile surface bears

His sweet weight. He tames the mad, or say, He frees
    them,

driving out the devils that held them and made them
    howl;

the unclean swine of Gadarra He drives into oblivion's
black waters; He feeds with only five loaves of bread
and a pair of little fishes, multitudes . . . O Lord,
You are our only meat and bread. The savor of life
is Yours. You nourish our bodies and feed our starving
    souls,
refreshing whoever partakes at Your holy banquet
    table.
The closed ears of the deaf You open to faintest
    whispers,
and mute tongues You can rouse from torpor to
    intricate speech.
The bedridden rise to their feet, exult in their new
    vigor,
pick up their beds, and dance in their joy through the
    city streets.
Even to those in Tartarus' gloom You have offered
    hope
of help, having forced the brazen bolts of the door
    and the hinges,
so the captive dead below, dazzled in sudden glare,
could cross that threshold again of the doorway,
    opened wide,
and stand in the golden light of God's eternal
    sunshine

that only once was darkened, as stars in the sky
    blinked
and the sun fled in sorrow and horror to leave a
    darkness
in which the earth shuddered in fear, bereft, dismayed.
And yet for that baleful cross, we sing in thanks and
    praise
of the victory of His passion, His wounds in which we
    were healed,
and His death that was no death. The ancient
    serpent's venom
is neutralized, its sting lethal no more, its hissing
throat silenced at last. The black stain of our guilt
is washed white in the crimson blood of God, our
    Savior.
His death is the death of death, for from Him the
    patriarchs learned
how to put on the garments of flesh and emerge from
    the tomb,
their dry ashes, their cold dust reassembled, recovered
in skin, and alive again, ascending to God's throne.
Glory to God the Father, the Judge of the dead and
    King
of the living! Glory to Him who sits at the Father's
    right hand.

From Him alone comes all our deserving, foe of the
    devil
and sin itself. Let us join to sing His praises, old
and young, and little children, matrons, maidens, and
    tots,
together in chorus. Let waters of rivers flow in a
    current
of praise, let the oceans dance in praise, and the rain
    rain down,
and the snow, in praise. Let day and night take turns
    in the heat
and cold to sing in Your honor in praise for ever and
    ever.

X

HYMN FOR BURIAL OF THE DEAD

We are incompatible elements joined,
mortal and immortal. They fuse
in the heat of the Lord's forge. Mankind
is fashioned thus. For a time it stays,

but the weld, which cannot hold, gives way,
for spirit yearns to rise to the sky
while flesh, which is earth, is drawn to obey
gravity's stern decree. We die,

and our contrary portions come undone,
but God is good and even yet
will not abandon anyone
who is His servant. Bodies rot

in congenial mire, and in the grave
the spirit is trapped that, lighter, fights

to rise, assert itself, and live.
For a time, the universe hesitates,

but flesh feels a sudden warming. Then
those cold bones twitch and corpses sigh,
reanimated, and rise again,
borne by the heavenly breezes, to fly.

Which of us would not groom the plot
of our departed? The shrouds, the myrrh
that preserves their corpses, are these not
the pains we take because we are sure

that Jesus' power will raise them? Saint
Tobias' father, Tobit the good,
refuses to eat his supper, can't
think of food, and is troubled: he should

perform the rites for the dead. For this
heaven rewards him well. His prize
is the cure of his blindness. Suddenly his
sight is restored and he blinks his eyes,

stunned by the light. The lesson is clear.
The ills of this world prepare us for

the joys of the next. We ought not fear
death, which we know is heaven's door.

This life is all decline and loss,
fading beauty, waning strength,
and wasting diseases, leaving us
piteous ruins, and yet at length

heaven shall make us whole, repair
our derelict frames, restore, improve,
and make us perfect everywhere.
Why do we mourn, then, those we love

with foolish lamentations? No,
no tears! What we bury here in the earth
is only the seed from which will grow
a fresh green plant. In this rebirth

we cannot doubt, for we believe
in heaven. We gaze down into a hole
in the gentle earth that we see receive
our dead, who issued, body and soul,

from the mouth of God. In faith and trust
we commit to Him who does not forget

His creatures these remains, that dust
the winds may scatter but God shall yet

revive and reassemble. We
will live again and breathe His breath.
Christ promised this eternity
to the thief on the cross, and we, in death,

shall lie in Abraham's bosom, sweet
with flowers' perfumes, as Lazarus does,
while Dives, the rich man, writhes in the heat
of hell, repenting what he was.

Help us, O Lord, to earn the right
to walk in that paradisaical
garden we come from, and consecrate
us to Your service, each and all.

Gather us from this exile, bring
us home again, we pray You. Save
us who, in a cemetery, sing
and sprinkle flowers on this grave.

XI
HYMN FOR CHRISTMAS

Having now reached the end of its track,
the sun begins its journey back.
This is the dawn of the year: the hours
of daytime will now increase, with the powers
of light and grace that attend the birth
of Christ, whom heaven gave to earth.
The planet, rejoicing, blushes, glad
so to be honored. O sweet lad,
child of a virgin and the Word
that the angel brought and Mary heard,
the wisdom of ages attended You
from the day of Your birth. You always knew
the order of all creation and
those things no mortal can understand—
how millennia passed and then
God deigned to show Himself to men,
redeem us from sin and moral blindness,

and save us through His loving kindness
from our idolatry and, worse,
the guile of the devil and his curse.
From the brink of the smoky pit, He snatched
us back. Our ruin, while He watched,
He could not suffer. He assumed
a mortal body, fragile, doomed.
To break death's chains, He came, and to bring
mankind back to our God and King.
It was upon this very day
that God put on our mortal clay.
The noble Virgin's time is near,
and — joy to the world! — her Child is here
whose infant tears perfume our air,
as foul as privies everywhere,
to the sweetness of mountain spikenard.
The rough turns smooth and every hard
boulder is gentled, covered in moss.
All nature exults! And the least of us,
the simplest herdsman, prays, and his sheep
and cattle adore the baby, asleep
in the rude cradle. All the nations
throughout the world for generations
numberless will declare their love

and faith in Him—but the children of
Isaac and Abraham refuse.
Maddened by Furies perhaps, the Jews
are obstinate, deny each sign
and wonder. This child of David's line
they shall one day confront on high
and then confess their error, cry
vain tears, as they hear the trumpet blare
for the end of days, for He will be there
judging each one according to
his proper deserts. And then, O Jew,
you shall be sensible of your loss,
and understand how, on that cross,
He suffered for us and there destroyed
mortality. From the awful void
of the tomb He saves us all, that black
abyss from which He brings us back.

XII

HYMN FOR EPIPHANY

Whoever would search for Jesus Christ
shall find Him. Only raise your eyes.
There is the sign of His glory, ablaze,
      a star in the skies,

surpassing in beauty and magnitude
even the sun. It warms the earth
with hope and faith, for the Lord is come
      in a human birth.

That star overhead proclaims the news,
blazoned on heaven for all to see.
By night and even by day, it burns
      in a constancy

no planet, comet, or constellation—
not even the Greater and Lesser Bears

that never set—can match. This shines
      and the universe stares,

amazed as it cuts through banks of clouds,
brighter than Sirius, brighter by far
than Venus, which it obscures in the East.
      This astonishing star

dazzled the soothsayers' cunning. Men
asked, "What means this glorious thing?
Can it betoken the coming of
      the exalted king

who was once foretold for every nation,
land and people?" Of Abraham's seed
He comes, from the father of all believers,
      who once agreed

to offer the life of his only son
as the measure of his devotion. Can
God do less in the sacrifice
      He makes for man?

Abraham's progeny, we read,
would equal the stars. And now we see
in the firmament on high how this
      has come to be,

in a single star outshining the rest.
From the royal house of David He springs
to take his rightful place among us
      as King of Kings.

The sceptered rod of Aaron bloomed
as a sign to Moses to show him his brother*
and the house of Levi were now God's priests.
      Here is another,

marking the way with a trail of light
to guide the three wise men who take
their gifts to the marvel, their newborn Master.
      There is no mistake,

for the portents are sure and clear. They fall
prostrate there in the rude room,

*Numbers 17:1–8.

with the frankincense for sweetness and bitter
    myrrh for the tomb.

The city of Bethlehem rejoices,
greater now than Athens or Rome,
for there is the Savior, the Son of the Father.
    This is the home

of God incarnate, the Thunderer's breath,
His testament, in witness whereof
the prophets of old have set their seals.
    The kingdom of love

at last is proclaimed through heaven and earth
from the depths of hell to the skies overhead.
Israel's King of Kings is born
    whom lesser kings dread—

which is why Herod decrees the death
of every infant boy. His mood
is black. His soldiers hear and obey:
    red rivers of blood

pour from Judaea's cradles. They snatch
suckling babes from their mothers' breasts,
hack at their helpless bodies, slash,
     and stab at their chests

in a barbarous frenzy. Herod's men
smash tiny heads on stone walls,
splashing blood and milky brains.
     It truly appalls,

and we look away but with no relief,
for on all sides are outrageous troubles.
A soldier is drowning a child in a barrel.
     He watches the bubbles.

The gurgling stops at last, and he smiles—
as we must, too, for these infant boys,
first martyrs of Christ, those earliest flowers
     cold wind destroys.

They are blooming still in the fields of the Lord.
At the sacred altar forever they play
with God's own crown and with palm fronds frolic.
     But Christ gets away,

escaping Herod's death-squads. Alone,
He is untouched, as Moses, too,
eluded the Pharaoh, who also raged
    at every Jew.

The zeal of the midwife saved that prophet,
or, say the Creator Himself it was
who rescued him who later would give us
    the tablet of laws.

The pattern is thus established, for Moses
slew the Egyptians and then set free
Israel's people, as Jesus Christ
    has saved you and me

from the stain of sin and the blackness of death.
Across the Red Sea, then, at Shur,
in the wilderness, for the people's thirst,
    Moses made pure

and sweet the brackish waters. And we
in baptism cleanse and purify.
They trusted a pillar of light to lead them,
    as three Magi

do, too. At last, they arrive at the promised
land where a Yeshua must win
at Jericho — as our Jesus does
      in His war with sin.

That Yeshua, at the Jordan's bank,
set out twelve stones so the ark of God
would not be wet and the priests who bore it
      could cross dry-shod.

Those dozen stones, one for each tribe
of Israel, set the pattern whence
we may derive the Apostle's number.
      A coincidence?

It is another sign that points
to the order of things in the Lord's plan.
The King of Kings was destined to come.
      Let every man

of the houses of Ephraim and Manasseh
and the other tribes revere and pray
to Him, and let the makers of idols
      all turn away

from the barbarous and smoke-begrimed
totems their fathers worshiped, stone
or metal or wood, rough-hewn or smooth.
        Jesus alone

is Master of Egypt, Greece, and Rome,
Judaea, and Persia. With every breath
let the quick, the sick, and the dead praise Him
        who has conquered death.

Poet, novelist, critic, and journalist DAVID R. SLAVITT has published more than fifty books. His translations include the *"Eclogues" and "Georgics" of Virgil, Ovid's Poetry of Exile, Seneca: The Tragedies,* volumes 1 and 2, and *The Fables of Avianus,* and he is co-editor (with Palmer Bovie) of *Plautus: The Comedies,* volumes 1–4.

LIBRARY OF CONGRESS CATALOGING-IN-PUBLICATION DATA

Prudentius, b. 348.

   [Cathemerinon. English]

   Hymns of Prudentius : The cathemerinon, or The daily round /
by Aurelius Prudentius Clemens ; translated by David R. Slavitt.

      p.   cm.

   Includes bibliographical references and index.

   ISBN 0-8018-5412-1 (hardcover : alk. paper)

   1. Prudentius, b. 348.—Translations into English. 2. Christian
poetry, Latin—Translations into English. 3. Hymns, Latin—
Translations into English. I. Slavitt, David R., 1935– . II. Title.

PA6648.P6A7   1996

874'.01—dc 20   95-51277